BLA

WAVE BOOKS   SEATTLE/NEW YORK

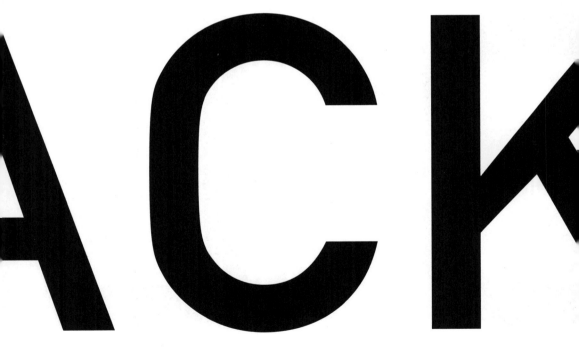

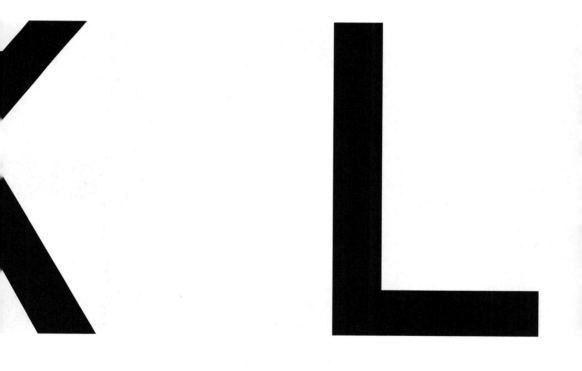

DOROTHEA LASKY

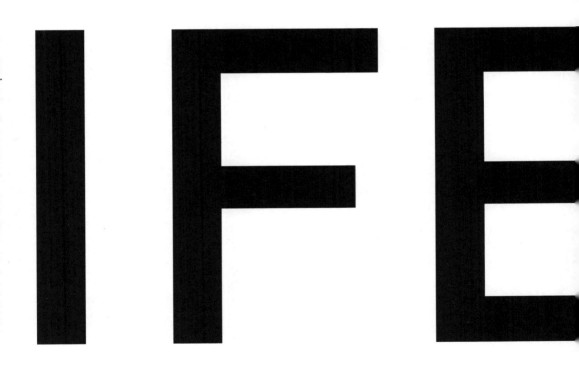

Published by Wave Books

www.wavepoetry.com

Wave Books titles are distributed to the trade by

Consortium Book Sales and Distribution

Phone: 800-283-3572 / SAN 631-760X

This title is available in limited edition hardcover

directly from the publisher

Library of Congress Cataloging-in-Publication Data

Lasky, Dorothea, 1978-

Black life / Dorothea Lasky. — 1st ed.

p. cm.

ISBN 978-1-933517-43-8 (pbk. : alk. paper)

I. Title.

PS3612.A858B47 2010

811'.6—dc22

2009036483

Designed and composed by Quemadura

Printed in the United States of America

9 8 7 6 5 4 3 2 1

Wave Books 021

FIRST EDITION

CONTENTS

BLA

''NO MILK / BLACK LIFE'' [LAURA SOLOMON]

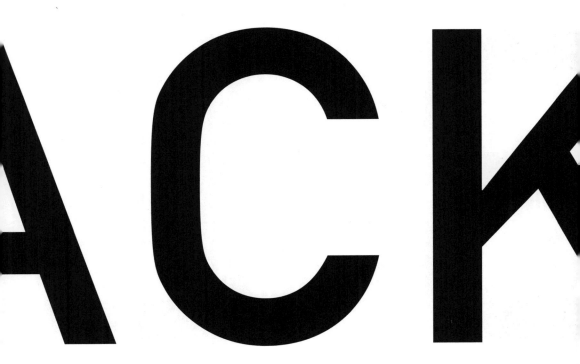

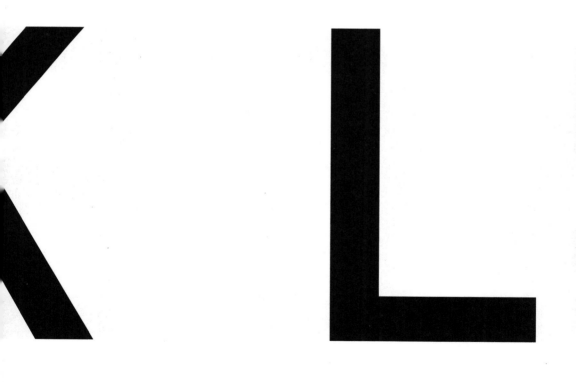

IFE

THE LEGEND OF GOOD JOHN HENRY

When my dad got Alzheimer's all the plants died

In the nursing home there are no plants

There is nothing to live for

Dogs circle the pink painted building

The orderly staff waits with the bleach

Asking me where the diapers are, I do not know

I haven't had a love in a very long time, a true love

One that makes you feel all jiggly inside

I haven't felt all jiggly inside since I don't know when

Still I will not go to work in a factory for machines

Art may want to be mechanized but I am not going to let it Goddamn it

Not gonna let it all be steel driver without my fist

Even the dead plants whisper to me to feed them

I feed them, the rabbits, and the dogs

I feed the babies bread toast, they are bald and wild

And strung out on life, the little igloos

Of their heads only cold when you think of all the possibilities of love
    like waiting

I am not what I once was, but who would want to be

Who would want to be the same throughout a life, read the same books

Drink the same tea, wear the same dress, go to the same movies

Oh how I would cry at the same man bent over the same actress in the
    same dark suit

Someone has died in that movie

O I have seen that one before

GO ON THERE, BOY

The boy there, he is the sun's son
Oh you might name him something
That name is nothing
His name is painting
The son of the sun is painting
The sun he is not the painting
We do not paint the sun
It lights the canvas that is the son
The light of the sun it is grave

O grave son, you write of many things
But before you write you bring me a cape
It is blue and it has rotted
Along with the rotted woman
Her name was Lori and her husband, Mark
He killed her to lie. O that the lie!
He loved the lie that lay there in his mind
The lie was something that lit the way

Little son, you go there on your way
I have taught you many things, so that you may be the painting
So be the painting, feel the love of it that is wet
The wet that rots like a fish who has been killed and we who killed it.

And we have killed it so now we eat
Let us eat! There is not much else
Worth opening the mouth for.
Not sex, not speaking, only food

That we put in it and then we talk.

But when we talk we talk of words that hold the painting

O let us hold the painting in our mouths

And chew it gently

Chew the killed woman gently

She has been lied to and then killed.

Let us kill her again, but in a different way.

TWO DOORS TO HELL

With each new day of being in love
I felt two doors opening out in front of me
One was a gate to something like hell
Another was the big expanse of green that is Life
I wanted to choose one but I couldn't
I had to write this
Unforgiving world who is so sure my rhetoric is mine
And not theirs
If I am anything I am the flattening of so many into one thing
That I am not powerful
At least not as myself
The gates of hell in front of me feel like an extending staircase of concrete
That falls below me
Into the great expanse which is Life
There is only Jesus waiting in my closet
Like he has been since I was 4 with his red eyes
I am convinced now that everything is going to be ok
Because I am happy now, still lonely
Because my heart is caught in something frivolous
But not so unhappy as before
Deadended into pigskin, a pigskin cave
Where I couldn't breathe
I can plant daffodils now among the heathens
Who are so replete in their belief in antiquity
That I can't help but think that they are the stupidest people on the earth
Although I know that's me
To feel so much for redness
Rushing forth on myself with a bitter sundering

With a soldering of smoking the skins in
And burning them so dark and crying
That they are no skins at all
I am in pain in this world
I have more than two options of good and evil
And this is horrible
To never be home
To be home in horror
And outside in the calm
And empty, among the soldiers
And other people I don't know
Who are so similar to me
Yet we can't speak
We don't speak about the same things
When I am wondering about the brain
They are thinking about art
Art is horrific, empty
It teaches the world to be mediocre
Making is not this
It fills up my house with a many splendid things
When the devil comes in he trips and
Gracefully gets up, but not before
He picks up the pretty thing that tripped him
And holds it in the light
Is this blue water, he asks me
Yes it is, I tell him
It is blue water
I have to be protected
Because I am so afraid

MIKE, I HAD AN AFFAIR

Mike, I had an affair
With Jakob Tushinea, the poet
It was in the cool light of dawn
That I came to him
From a long journey
As what was between us was true love
Although he was too young to see it.
I peered into his crevices
And upon his bed I peered into more
Like the kind of things that the monsters make.
He was a monster, no
He was not a monster, Mike
His skin was soft and wild
And when he smiled
I was a bit on fire
He closed the papers on the shelves
The foxes of the morning
That raise their horrible whiskers
And when the affair was over
I said good-bye to him,
But he was never able to truly say good-bye to me.
You know I am a great woman
I am a great woman, I have the wiles
That make the poet
But I am also gentle
And when I kiss a man I really mean it
Have you felt this too, upon my kisses
That I gave to you in the nightsky
As your eyelashes hung over the moon?
Or were you too young to see it too,
My little feverish butterfly

JAKOB

I am sick of feeling

I never eat or sleep

I just sit here and let the words burn into me

I know you love her

And don't love me

No, I don't think you love her

I know there are clouds that are very pretty

I know there are clouds that trundle round the globe

I take anything I can to get to love

Live things are what the world is made of

Live things are black

Black in that they forgot where they came from

I have not forgotten, however I choose not to feel

Those places that have burned into me

There is too much burning here, I'm afraid

Readers, you read flat words

Inside here are many moments

In which I have screamed in pain

As the flames ate me

FAT

Sometimes anorexia is all you have left

When the fat surrounds you

Like blubber from a lamb

That has been defatted and fatted again

By so much sadness

You are not sure where its skin ends

Bhanu Kapil screams THERE IS NO SUCH

THING AS SKIN in my ear every time

I listen to her recording when I am alone

I have never seen her in the flesh

But to see a poet in the flesh is to not know anything

To see an engineer in his flesh is nothing

I have written poems about the flesh of scientists

But nothing in their science speaks to me about my art

I have wandered for six days with no bread, drank lemon water

Went running for a hundred miles until the sun

Shot purple streaks everywhere

It was beautiful to be a skeleton that everyone in my culture loved

I wore the most elegant clothes and draped my bony fingers

Over the same book I had written when I was fat

Except that the book seemed so big in front of my little bones

I love people in this life

The thing I love the best is being skinny

Because thinness can't yell at you

Can't turn its head away

You only go towards death

Like it is a very small detail

On a long path of forgiving
I will never forgive myself
For living in such a disturbing way
As the way in which I lived this life
For all eternity
Like this poem, it is so fat and useless
And no one kisses this paper
And in the end no one will protect
This paper from the rain

WHEN YOU WANT TO READ, YOU CAN'T READ

When you want to read, you can't read

When you want to love, the people are never there

The bird on the wire is full of fire

And he is fire red, but he is never there

My father says there is a house he used to go to

Where his brother and six old men would give him a bit of change

I ask him who I am and he says I am his wife

Daddy, I am your wife in this world and the next

I went down the pit of fire and found you are my husband

I wanted to write a story about it, or a novel even

I wanted to light the whole thing up but it wasn't there to burn

I cut the fire with my knife

It was a fire sword

That I swashed about the world, O how I swashed

The great fire sword that lit the sky

I lit the sky

I think I was the sun

That was in me all along, though I never knew it

But who can know what they will become?

They can only live as if they will never know it

Well, who could live a whole life

Always knowing they will never belong

POEM TO AN UNNAMEABLE MAN

You have changed me already. I am a fireball

That is hurtling towards the sky to where you are

You can choose not to look up but I am a giant orange ball

That is throwing sparks upon your face

Oh look at them shake

Upon you like a great planet that has been murdered by change

O too this is so dramatic this shaking

Of my great planet that is bigger than you thought it would be

So you ran and hid

Under a large tree. She was graceful, I think

That tree although soon she will wither

Into ten black snakes upon your throat

And when she does I will be wandering as I always am

A graceful lady that is part museum

Of the voices of the universe everyone else forgets

I will hold your voice in a little box

And when you come upon me I won't look back at you

You will feel a hand upon your heart while I place your voice back

Into the heart from where it came from

And I will not cry also

Although you will expect me to

I was wiser too than you had expected

For I knew all along you were mine

HOW TO SURVIVE
IN THIS WORLD

Whatever you do don't feel anything at all
When that big mammoth of a man comes inside of you
Don't say anything at all
When your friends call you drunk and are annoying
Because they do nothing with their lives
Just smile and say that's life
There is a lot to be sad about
But no point in feeling that sadness
In a world that has no capacity
To take your sadness from you in a kind way
Instead it steals it from you and turns it into
Gambling or other sorts of useless endeavors
Like also talking on the phone, which is useless
I got so mad having to show up to him
After he had come inside of me
He pretended I didn't know he was crazy
Had bad taste in music
Was a mediocre poet
And the worst part was that he was really an atheist
Atheists are all over this world and they are such idiots
To think they are the ones who know what is really going on in the world
I know what's going on in this world
When I hear Puffy's sweet voice I just pretend
I don't know he is a saint, but he is
He is a saint that Puffy
And his voice is a midnight I'd like to walk into forever
But instead I pretend he is nothing
With that rose water poured all over him
His coat an aching shade of white

IT FEELS LIKE LOVE

When he and I are together, it just feels like love
And when we are talking and laughing together
It feels like love
And when we are hugging and going places together
It just feels like love, it feels like love
And his eyes on me and the way he looks
And what he says and the way I feel
And the things he does and the feelings I get
And the songs that play and my mind a racing
And the Spring racing before us and the sun and moon
And the low light of the evening
With the dark trees silhouetted and the birds aflame
It just feels like love
It really does
I don't know
I must have said it all wrong

POEM TO MY EX-HUSBAND

Dear husband, I tried to write you an e-mail
But I didn't have the right address
My husband, I love you so much
Will you be mine forever
I know you are married now
Does that matter
I can still remember holding hands
I bought a purse
And I remember the walks that we took
There were black butterflies all around us
I was twenty-one or twenty-two, O darling
Your black black hair was coal black
I slept next to it every night
And then we got a car together
And then it was over
My sweet baby you were always there
You always
Loved me, in the shower you would bathe me
And feed me later in bed spaghetti or something else
And when I got sick
You were the one who went to the all-nite store
Dear husband, I miss you so much
Strange men who write bad poems
Tell me I disrupt their wives
I don't even think they have a brain, let alone a dick
I would disturb nothing about them
If I ran into them on the train I wouldn't even notice
How bland their jokes and voice

I would never disrupt your wife
My sweet sweet
I would never take away anything you have made
In the fear you have made me
What I am forever
And I will always love you
No matter what you do
Or I do
My heart will yearn for yours through all eternity
And you will never get away from me
I will haunt you even when I am dead
I will wear plastic horseshoes on my ghostly suit
They will be striped, multicolored
I will be protected from the sun
That blinds me from you
You will have no breath
That I do not take with you
You will have no movement that will not be my own
You will gesture and it will be my gesture
That guides, when words
Leave your mouth they will be my words
Your words are my words
I say them and they say you
All that I can never make in the movement
Of my voice and arm
And crowned in lights
I place your moving mouth next to a red drill
And together we go to someplace like a beach
Where they give us things we need, like life

15

SOME SORT OF TRUTH

When my dad first started to die
All my mom could remember
Was the time he kicked her out
After they first started dating
So that he could go play golf
It is the sort of thing we all remember
When we feel death upon us
I remember he died twice
And once in my dream
I just had to see him all nursed and swaddled as if he were sleeping
But he wasn't sleeping
I stood in the white light of the nursing home bathroom
With the sun spilling everywhere on me
And tried to talk to him, but never, he'd never listen
People don't always listen to you when they are dead
But that's not sad
I get tired
And I don't listen to one Goddamn thing you are saying
But that is because most of the time you bore me
And when I am finally asleep it is really nice just to dream
I have seen a lot of things in this life
But one thing I saw most readily
Was that despite his eternal heartbreak
And girlish silliness
Mike's face was kind of sweet, a sweet wind
He is going to think it is weird that I put him in this poem
But I don't think it is weird that I put him in this poem

BLACK NIGHT

Black night I am in the plane
And the horizon can be seen as dark green and pink
I am wearing all black except for my teal bracelets
And my hair is a pinkish shade of red
No not pinkish, an auburn that it always was
The plane is soaring through the dark night
And I am not
I always fly alone
Because I gave up several chances to be married
And now I just take it all right
They say that the people love me out there
I can't imagine
What me soaring in the black night as just a thing
I know that when they might get close to my face
They would stop their love
Ghoul I am when you are close to me
As my niceness does never end
That is the surprise
That the kindness was not an affect, but a choice
And that kindness in its entirety is very freakish
And weird, the real kind.
But still I leave things open like wood
Sculptured wood pieces that adorn my every move.
I don't even know how to write a poem anymore.
Rattly rattly is my voice, what it once was
When I was just a girl, I used to think
Of what it could be and now it is nothing
I am nothing

The people look upon me, I am so black
Burned black, my black face
I mean real black, the dark kind, the night
Not the word for how we divide each other
Not white, black, or red, yellow
I mean black, the darkness
That we all succumb to or if we don't, we never live
I mean love, the dark kind
That is so all-encompassing you can't ever get away
When I speak to you, you can't ever get away from me, my love
As much as you might want to, so you give in
Night of ghouls and spirits that I succumb to
So that you may succumb more fully
Black night I am in
Still soaring, by myself
The warm November lights
Glittering below me like a pale escape

ME AND THE OTTERS

Love makes you feel alive
Johnny my animal you have no idea
How beautiful you are to me in the morning
When it is 5 a.m. and I am lonely
Everyone is dying around me
I eat spinach bread to keep my sanity, I am
Like Lisa in the mental unit with my father
I am Muriel who throws tables
I play blackjack with the clowns
Oh yes I do all that for a salad
Your black hair is better than a piece of fate
I find in the sky when I am looking
45,000 miles above the earth
For things that make it all worthwhile
I do this for you but you will never know
How dear you are to me
You chop leaves in your house in New York City
Dream of glamorous women and even too they are great
No one will ever love you like I do that is certain
Because I know the inside of your face
Is a solid block of coal and then it too
Something that is warm like warm snow
I hold the insides of you in my palm
And they are warm snow, melting even
With the flurries glutted out of the morning
When I get on the plane the stewardess tells me to let loose
My heart, the man next to me was the same man as last week
Whoever those postmodernists are that say

There is no universal have never spent any time with an animal
I have played tennis with so many animals
I can't count the times I have let them win
Their snouts that were wet with health
Dripping in the sun, then we went and took a swim
Just me and the otters, I held them so close
I felt the bump of ghosts as I held them.
There is no poem that will bring back the dead
There is no poem that I could ever say that will
Arise the dead in their slumber, their faces gone
There is no poem or song I could sing to you
That would make me seem more beautiful
If there were such songs I would sing them
O they would hear me singing from here until dawn

THE ANIMAL

The pigeon man ate my heart out
I saw him sitting there but he didn't see me
As he fed the pigeons
Three pigeons on each leg and one on his shoulder
My father sleeps, his one head out the window
I cannot hear the sound of thunder in this wind tunnel
I cannot speak
The things I have seen while giving flight
To a love that was underrated
My heart belongs to a lion
I love his pelt and covet his heart
O animal, your heart is wise beyond your years
I cut your paw and you tell me in a whisper
To never leave this place
So that's what I do
But really I want to know
If you will throw that fat stake upon my heart
And give me something that is worth saving
Like the gospel of lions or worse yet, gazelles
That speak so gracefully within the wind
I touch that gazelle speak and it is as pink as day
I leave it upon the ocean, that pinkish bird that speaks to me
I let it fly upon the palms, O let it fly
My pinkish speech that I once lost but now I know
Will always be a part of me if I only stop to listen

THE BRACELET

A big bracelet is like a big pain

That is the thing people don't understand

That it is the pain that makes you get

All the things you never get

Except you get them all at once

I was hungry but not for prayer

Why shelves? Shelves have more room

For putting food on

You tore the shelves down

And hit my father for no reason other than he's sick

That's pain

To hear your father scream

And to know he is being beaten

Undulating in red plastic swirls

That Sobral makes

The big brown and black paint

That cover the thing

I wear that bracelet on my arm

I read poems and they are to cover my bracelet

I don't get my book published and then I do

Men never love me, oh what's the use

To have that love that I never get

Except all at once

I would like to snuff out all my thoughts

I would like to wear one long bracelet as long as my arm

No one ever reads a bracelet

I would be so secret in my hiding

No one would hear me laugh and say 'Oh I love your laugh'

O what do they know of laughter
Those bitter women who secretly beat my father
On a long dark trellis on the rocks in the morning
They swarm the ocean with their deceit
And even the gods have had enough of them
Those things that made me
I was never made
From things I cannot be
I never run
From things I have not become
I will never swim
On a lake in the winter with frogs
Those frogs are my enemies
They croak out revenge to all who will listen
O they croak out fire, but no one ever listens

EMILY D

Dear love, you tell me of Emily D
Who locked herself in the closet, oh did she lock
Her heart away, it was sailing
Across the great oceans with blue night, I knew her once
When I went to that house where she did the writing
And I saw the insanity that makes a man
I am insane
But only in my heart
My mind is lost forever in its iniquity
It rations the deed and dead like the rest of us
Do we even know the lesson we are left to learn?
Are things not fully spaced, the heart it did fold
I felt myself lessening, my mind was locked
Upon one door in one house
I left my rat heart on the table
I took my bird mouth to the door
I let out a cat scream
It echoed through the halls
But they didn't hear me, the house was full of fire
The smoke is blinding, but then it is the fire
That burns you, you have no mind
And you lessen within yourself
And you don't go awry as much as you leave
And hide in another universe where things don't burn
Did Emily D even have a shot?
She had one chance lost and locked in fate
I guess that is what we all have
One chance locked in fate
A fixed thing we can't ever move

ARS POETICA

I wanted to tell the veterinary assistant about the cat video Jason sent me
But I resisted for fear she'd think it strange
I am very lonely
Yesterday my boyfriend called me, drunk again
And interspersed between ringing tears and clinginess
He screamed at me with a kind of bitterness
No other human had before to my ears
And told me that I was no good
Well maybe he didn't mean that
But that is what I heard
When he told me my life was not worthwhile
And my life's work the work of the elite.
I say I want to save the world but really
I want to write poems all day
I want to rise, write poems, go to sleep,
Write poems in my sleep
Make my dreams poems
Make my body a poem with beautiful clothes
I want my face to be a poem
I have just learned how to apply
Eyeliner to the corners of my eyes to make them appear wide
There is a romantic abandon in me always
I want to feel the dread for others
I only feel it through song
Only through song am I able to sum up so many words into a few
Like when he said I am no good
I am no good
Goodness is the not the point anymore
Holding on to things
Now that's the point

MEMORIES

My dad did not remember the time he spent in the hospital
It was like much of it never happened
God is the thing that sees everything happening all at once
Death is when you don't
See it
You don't see everything happening
You are small
I was angry
At him
My dad would never read this poem and know exactly what I mean
I never get recourse for the good things I do
I am only a clear piece of resin, encased in bubbles
The bubbles are multicolor, they ring
Around everything, even the moon.
I did not want to know death, but I knew death
I did not want to know dying, but it uttered from me
Like a black bird you can't keep away
You can't keep God away no matter how hard you try
He is there to link it all together
Things go away fast
Your brain is not what you take it for
Let your brain look at everything
I am so glad it came to me
That brain I didn't even know was there to save me
From the thing I would not remember
O green sun that was there in September
The brown woods with their bitter heads
O olive green lake with blue birds
I will never stop looking at you
I am so glad you came around

I AM A WILD BAND

I am a wild band
That is going fast at you
Catch me catch me
Catch me Lord
I am a hot little thing that likes to kiss you
Kiss me kiss me
Or if you can't kiss me, then you can catch me
Wild sound that goes around you
I am a shell that crashes in you
And makes a sound within you
Help me help me
When I shutter in you, I break within you
It hurts me to break within you
You will forget this as I break within you
You will enjoy the sound of me breaking in you
It is me you are breaking in you
For your pleasure I break and shutter
Please remember that this hurts me
I am a moving train that crashes
That spins across a night highway and then crashes
Into a deer
And then the deer goes through me
Save me save me I have broken
But I do not know what for
Except to give you pleasure
I don't know what else what for
So you can sleep, my little babies
In the white cold night
O the night, in me in me
I hold the night within me
O it hurts as it breaks inside of me

THAT ONE WAS
THE ODDEST ONE

That Robbie Wood is so weird

He seriously makes me want to fuck his brains out

Oh fuckable man, why do you have to do and say such

Strange things? Why if they were only all so weird

I would fuck them all night, their dicks hanging out of their mouths

When I am done, little red mouths with no words

Instead no one is so weird

They have muscles

I write these poems instead of sitting in a bed

Sweaty all day

With men who are truly fuckable

I fuck men with muscles, brains, a heart

Men who might listen at times

Not one of them tells jokes about chameleons and armadillos

Like sweet Robbie Wood, who calls me out of the blue

And the one first time I saw him smile, I felt as if

I had been punched in the gut

Oh I know how that one student felt who was in love with me

I say weird things

Weirdness is such a turn-on

EVEN DIRTY BIRDS

Sun on the shadows, even dirty birds are nice when they brush up against you
Like the pigeons in the park when they come whirling at you they are nice
To feel their wings and necks against you, like wind only better
Because they are living
Grey birds because they are dirty
With city soot, the smokestacks
Of living in a sour time, the way that we breathe so
In every city legend we work
Too fast to be part machine but only part of it
That we are machines only in that we are not birds
I am part of this world but I am not
Of this time and place, when you look at me
You can see it in my eyes that I am not
What you thought I was, and when you stand next to me
You will feel my aura is not the aura of this time but a timeless time
That is always new because it is water and air
And when I speak, it is a new voice but it is not a new voice
No, it is an old one, no it is present so
That you find yourself in love with me
Well who could blame you, I can't stop you
From loving a ghost of yourself that was willing to speak
Of living things that you so readily had forgotten when you yourself so was
    so living so living so that you forgot how to breathe and you died
I will not let you die, no
So there are ghosts that are not me but that I am a reflection of
In that I am living, water, and air, part lime in that I am a woman
But I am not a woman so much so that I am air

And air that breathes through you giving you a home that I will never
    take away
I will never take this home away, soft bed that is my voice
And hot chili in the dinner I make for you
You have come back from working all day with coal and ice
Come back, I will take you back to what you once knew

YELLOWBIRD

When the words you say are valued

They are more important words

Why do people think I'm weird?

I'm not weird

Constantly looking over my shoulder, the swan

Gets his big feathers in me, they are not my feathers

That soak the morn in their exactitude

Half askew the inner worlds of the dead are

Before they reach our world, which is one thing

I saw the moon rising and knew it was full of white feathers

Except you see the rocks, they are bumpy and silent

So many things have flown through them, but what they contain so

Like love, I so did contain

Many voices

They weren't mine

I'm not weird, like death

I am a turquoise woman who is gentle

O gentle me the men in suspenders

O gentle moon that rose so

I was yellow flower rose in the sun

So bright it could be seen from Mars until here

O pretty moon, your fire flowers

Are so weird for everyone to see

But don't change yourself, fire flower

They do not know what they say

SOME PEOPLE DO IT

Some people do it but they don't do what they can't done
Some people do it but they can't
They can't do it They can't do it
They want to do it
But they don't know the score
They don't know the way to form
What it is that is inside
They hide that side
Because that side makes no table
Makes no face of flesh to hide the table with
I sit at the table with those who can't done
You are the table of those who can't did
I can't did I can't did
Make what was in me shine and see
What it was I once was that was worth seeing
I see lots of things I can't know
I can't do what I can't did, the flame did
The flame does go, out of your mouth, it is a red fire
Into the red fire, the mouth does go
When we are together, it is hot between us, a mouth did
The heat is what we once were, what we could do
I could do it I could do it
Feel what we once were
I felt it what we once did:
The birds chirping in the moon
I am not what I once was
Oh that I was once was
What we all were

Oh that I once did
What we all did
Just for the sake
Of what we do
I know what we do
We do did, we did come
To see what we all did
That was worth seeing
I did did, take the ribbon do
I took the red ribbon, put it in my mouth
My mouth knew the ribbon
Saw what it once was
Ribbon gone once were
What we all come
That it once was
What we all knew
Oh what I did
For you to do
Is take the ribbon out
Put it in my mouth

THINGS

There are things leftover, things we discard

Contact lens cases, eyedrops, tampons, old tissues filled with tears

I once emptied urine into a pot I was pissing in

Put the cum-filled condom into the trash, O cum-filled condom

You will never be a baby, only to discard like earth

We discard dead babies, their heads buttery and soft

By the time they reach the ground

Blood and water we leave those too, and fruit juice

Fruit juice we empty down the drain, and flowers, purple and worn

I once threw six love letters out the window of a moving car

And the love they belonged to I was never quite taken with enough to lose

Kisses I threw out to children because I love them

Love children in that they are the fire of the world that keeps me breathing

No, when I say that, it is not for effect

Not for some ironic gesture to say I love children

You should be less cynical, world that I live in

That throws itself out with every misstep

War you're too good for, poem I wrote in the bathroom

Laundry that got soiled just right after washing with the day's rain

Snot that got all over the sheets for no reason other than it is cold, cold
    outside

It's cold outside, can you feel it?

Have you turned yourself so way up you cannot feel it, well then wake up

I do not think you know what it is you keep, world heart beating like a bird
    in the sun

Who is warm despite itself, despite the death or humor that will overtake it

Dorothea, the bird might say to you, I love you anyway

Even though your head is not fire like you thought, but a gentle meat that
    lets go

From what holds it back until it is nothing

Fire world, you will say back, you are nothing

I thought that I would become

That one day I was dreaming I thought of some other thing I have never seen

But will never see, because it is not the time to

See what we all hope with, the thing that is empty

And the bird will say nothing to this, he is bald and wise

And he will rise from the tree made of tea

He will go speak to someone who cares

I do not care but neither does the bird

He was not made to care and neither was I

The burnt sun was made to care, so it cares for you

So look at it lovingly, stroke its hot shoulders, the bright light coming out
of it was made for you

And sit in the bright light, and bask in its beauty

Bright sun, sun that was made for you,

Warm hot belly, white-hot love that was made for you

EVER READ A BOOK
CALLED *AWE*?

Have you ever read a book called *AWE*?

I have. I wrote it. That's my book.

I wrote that book. I wrote that one.

Some people read it. They said,

We will make your book.

I said, Really? I love you.

They said, We love you, too.

I said, Good then

I will love you forever.

They said, Great! And looked scared.

Some people I love

Don't love me

Others love me

That's good

When you sit in a landscape of snow

And you're a bird, that's Awe

When you look over a big green field

And the dead soldiers lie all around you, that's Love

That's Love and Awe.

Say it

That's Love and Awe.

There is nothing better.

Or if there is

Then I don't care

I LOVE A MATHEMATICIAN

I love a mathematician

Not a man who lives by himself in a minivan, which one is he?

Masturbating to my picture on the internet, just like the fat one in the
   basement

Masturbating and masturbating, oh how I love that

And would love to drain the blood from his face too

In person

O how I would identify with the sickly nature of love

And sweet sticky kisses

That never go away.

Reader.

By now you know

That I am scary and sad

But that I am not scared to be

I am scared to get killed by the river

But that is because it has happened before

When you make 500 dollars a week like some people

Then you can fly off to Hawaii whenever you want to

I am just living on credit now

I am just living on my good name

THANK YOU TO
JASON M. HELMS

Thank you to Jason M. Helms

Who for a short while

Saved me from the loneliness of the black night

In which I slept and woke

And there was no end to the sleeping and waking

And to say thank you that he did not lie to me

As some men are prone to do

But gave me the whole thing straight

So that I am not embarrassed to say his name

Jason M. Helms

Or that we met in the summertime

When the grasses were high near the sun

Opossums wander and scurry

Opossums wander and scurry with love, they are not cute

But likable in their strangeness

To thank a stranger is strange but I do so anyway

Because he is a child

Because that is what they think of me

THE DEVIL AND THE INFINITE NIGHT

Sometimes I get so scared that I believe I have been possessed by the devil

So that I scream and holler and try to push him out of me

I wake up in bed and he is standing over me with his yellow eyes

He doesn't know my name but he knows me

Cause he used to possess my sister and I would see him in her

Now she is a nun

I watch youtube videos of exorcisms and in one I banned myself from
watching it as soon as I did

The woman crept backwards on the stairs, yelling with her eyes out like
pitchforks

The scary thing was that I didn't see her face when she got to the top of
the stairs

And only saw the upturned face with the devil's eyes coming down them.

Still I think it is sometimes

But the devil is not murder

If a man murdered me I would be so scared

But it would be a living scared

That I would die and the sun would rise despite of me

When I think of death by the devil I only think of suns

Rising infinitely into space like some nightmare

But a nightmare you can't get out of because it is the night

That is all encompassing

I get all encompassed by the night every day

People think I am very friendly and innocent

I spend every day inside this house being the creepy thing they couldn't handle

If they really saw deep into my eyes they couldn't handle me

Once they could see the darkest part of me surrounding them

The blackest part of my eyes in front of them, a sun that never sets

VERY VIVID AND HORRIBLE DREAMS

I had very vivid and horrible dreams

All night long when my mother was trying to kill herself

In one dream, there was an assailant who had lined the steps of my walk-up

With forty versions of the same exact piggy bank I got when I was four

And then throughout the dream he kept looking for me so that he could kiss
    me, but I was so unkissable

In the next dream I just showed up in Seattle and Monica and Travis had to
    deal with me

Patiently, they put on the tube and made me some bread

Until I abruptly left in a white truck

And sailed through the sky to a large amphitheatre filled with idiots

There was a blonde there, a beautiful blonde

The kind of woman I have always wanted to be

And of course my mother loved her better than me

"She is an illusion" I cried and struck the blonde across the face

Until her dimples melted into the thin air

Then I screamed and hollered

And threw my cape upon myself

And went flying through the hall in extremely graceful pirouettes

So that they could all not help but smile

At how sweet I was

But also all-powerful, too

I woke up and I knew all the dead people

That had haunted my life from birth until that period

I knew the men in boardrooms that had been fighting a different kind of war

Only to one day die as frail as they came

Only to one day die! I left this life and went into the next
Where I was myself, but a skinny self
A better self
A more ferocious self that no one expected of me
Not even my dead mother lying there
Telling me it was all my fault that we had been born in a dustbin

GREEN

[FOR NOELLE KOCOT]

Green feathers fell everywhere
The dogs went wild around me
All of the children who were sitting there
Their hair turned and was white-tipped
And the hair was dipped in white like lightning
Or the hair really was lightning, I was mistaken
"This is the answer!" we all said
No, but we were mistaken
That was not the answer
We were confused
We had slept in our clothes and couldn't remember
So I wandered for many months among mountains
I took the work of Jason M. Helms upon me
And sat by a waterfall
Trying to understand
What it was I already did
"Green" I said
And he smiled loudly
"Green" we said
And took a break

BLACK LIFE

You are born and it is to a black life
Full of abuse and strange things
Monsters come up to you as soon as you enter
Mouths asunder and fingers thrashing
Dark purple monsters that are so full of blood
They are a darkish bluish red

You grow and it is to a black life
That you consider
All around you is death and atheism
All around you are people who have misinterpreted science
For their own gain
There are nuns, but they are the nuns of the air

You die and it is from a black life
That you die from
You leave this one and go into the next
Where nothingness surrounds and evaporates
With the ease of something
That has done this sort of thing before

I leave and I am a black life
I leave you cause you didn't need me after all
And I want to
Be what you made me to be
But you never really made me
This life made me
This thing that I am

TORNADO

I remember he was bent down
Like a whirlpool
I was yelling at him
He looked scared and backed away
Another time, I squinted my eyes to see
And he said I looked ugly
The funny part was when
My sister asked me where he went to
And I just didn't know
He just disappeared one day into nothing
I am rotting and rancid
Each day, rotting, but I am water, too
I am a watery nymph that is hot and wet
Like a wetted beast
I saw the man walking, hunched over
And thought it was him
"Father!" I yelled after the man
Who was hunched, he was going somewhere
He turned but the face was green
It is a black life, but I don't want to die
I don't want to die, I don't ever want to die
Goddamn you, don't you shoot me in my sleep
Let me rot on this earth forever
Like a carrot I will be everything God can't see
Oh what do I mean
God can see everything
I mean the angels, I mean the half-gods
I mean the flowers, don't ever let them see me live forever
Don't you ever let them see
That I am all root here in the ground

OWN LIFE

Eric, you have your own life

What other thing is like that—a hat!

And in a hat I have found that I could wear one

What people don't understand about being a genius is

Is that it is hard

It creeps inside of you and you can't relate

The world is the thing you cannot master

You really can't

You try to work for people

You let the people down

I AM A POLITICIAN

I am a politician

Just watch:

I will be very nice to you

But when I turn around I will write the creepiest poems about you that
   have ever been written

Or worse yet,

I will write nothing about you at all

And will instead

Write about the water cascading endlessly in the ocean

Full of flowers and lovers at their very best

That is because I am a politician

That I do it this way

And am necessarily political

But only when it matters

Like when I am fed

Or better yet

I do care about your schooling, your hospitals

I work my life like I am Dorothea Dix

Because that one day when I learned about her big heart

I realized there was more we shared than the same first name

But shared the reason that we love those who suffer

Simply because they can't love themselves

O birds who suffer in the long September morn

You sing to me because I am one of the people

And I hear you because I am not one of anything

But a lone soul that was born to speak.

But speak of political things or strange endeavors

Or calculated finery?

I only speak of myself when I smile at you

And when I smile at you

That is the scariest thing of all I could ever do

SAD

I am just so very sad
And this is not for some gesture
That I tell you about this sadness now
No one loves me
I don't love them either
There are things to be done in the world
And I do them
Only out of a place of despair
That I make these things happen
Listen
I was born a separate human than you
But that does not mean I do not understand you
Or cannot accept you fully in my own way
I have been a lot of places
Most of them in my mind
But places nonetheless
That I have gone
I was meant to go there
Why?
Because there is no one else to left
From this place we have all not left
And what's the use?
There is none
Except that there are rocks and stone
In the universe's vast landscape
That are misunderstood
Left for dead
Because they can't be seen
So I sail through the black night
While you sleep snugly

And rescue the forgotten things
So you don't have to
And place them gently in your dream
My sweet, you walk past them hurriedly
But I know you will notice them eventually in your own way

LITTLE MORE
THAN A PLAYER

For a long time I believed I was more than a player
But then I realized I wasn't more
Than a person who wanted to get so far away from love until it hurt
Men are indispensable
But the specifics of them are not
Anything to write home about
They walk and talk and make me money
Take my money
Smoke cigars, read me books
I find their gentleness annoying most of all
It is not so much that I am good at any part of loving them
It is just that I make them believe so fully that I will love them forever
That they rise into the baby kingdoms of themselves and do my bidding
I am a player
But that's no crime
To go on mercilessly not loving anybody for all eternity
Or not believing in anything
Cause of what I can't feel
I am a player but so is everyone
Your mom, your dad
It is one big game that we play
When we call out love
And when that final day comes to die
We will all be the biggest players of all
Scooting across the floor in our blue suits
While everyone sniffs and sobs

At our lives long gone
We were always gone
All of us who live on this earth
We were always lit up red on this earth, long gone
I am long gone every time I believe that some man
Might bring me to salvation
He does little more than bring me to the muscle of him
I do little more than act out my great escape
Of when I can finally leave this earth an unchanged fellow
A wild kid, a nighttime baby full of delicious and ungenerous sparks

IT'S A LONELY WORLD

It's a lonely world
Hi everybody
It's Dorothea, Dorothea Lasky
I have done something very wrong and
I am so very sorry about it
"You have done a very bad,
Very bad job" my old boss says
In his Honda
As I take his dick in my mouth—it is all I have left
Men that look like surfers read at the local bar
As my old boss empties me out of his car
Without so much as a kiss
I see a pretty girl in purple lipstick—she is me
I have done something so wrong that my mother can die from it
Laura walks across the universe in a mumbling tongue
And in her stupor she doesn't necessarily connect my name with my face
I have acted in such a worse way it made
My baby win his law school parade
And they hoisted him up, even the girls did
With a big party full of balloons
There is something so wrong with me
That I make the baby's diapers even in my sleep
Because they need making
The baby comes home and falls gently down the stairs
So that we can see his head cracking like a watermelon
All that pressure built up like a haze of stars
I am red-mouthed again and I go out the door
There is a sun setting, with a halo around it

I tell people, who are listening to me, that that sun is God
But they never believe me, they only listen
They only believe what they are taught to believe
Which is to believe in nothing
Which is what they were taught when they were born

NUNS

I felt sad watching my mom among the nuns

Like in the same way I felt sad watching

My husband walk away from me

Backwards through the rain

He was in a movie

I was in a movie

About sadness

We were horrible to each other

Some things that hold people together are not love

There are ungenerous ways we make ivory statues in churches

There are ways we cut glass up to make paintings out of light

To hang in churches

That are not so good after all

There are a hundred places in this country where a hundred women with
   white hair sit

And dream of the afterlife, Christ!

Christ, that afterlife is not so good

I can think of my birthday body on a hot day

Burning into the earth like a rotten angel

All done up in makeup my sister put on me

As sterile as we see ourselves in death

The way my husband lived so sterile

In his face and hands, never letting himself give over

To the great spirits of the heavens

Now and then I touch a lover

And think of him, so pure and waxy

His body held over by nuns at the church

Near where his parents live

I don't think he'll ever be anything

At all
I don't think he'll ever amount to anything at all
But a sexless body in the sun with nuns
Oh too, I still love him
I was once so sexless in the midst of love
When I was young
And was not sticky with a thousand men
In the afterlife
Their dead hands aching on me like a million breasts
All piled on top of heads
On the top of hands and feet
All of us so millennial in our exacting pulchritude
Piling on top of each other, no longer one author among many
But one author as many
One author as full of everything
Of many as a grand God
Would be at the time of the apocalypse
Of the great judgment
Even here and there women who would be nuns
In another life look at me cross-eyed
Unable to see the similarities that erase us
My love says he is surprised at how much
We use the word iteration when we are together
We do so, he and I, to signify the similarities that are not so similar
Still caught in being one thing, forever entwined
He should not be surprised, no he should be
He was never one thing, similar among many
He was one singular thing into the stars, I can't ever reach him
I go running after him, I will never be bored
To find him when I find him, soft skin, and then always rushing

To a new fire he finds, always rushing, smoking, lit up

He thinks we are all iterations of each other, or someone once told him that

Someone once told him that, and she wasn't wise

No no you were not wise, girl, the opposite of a nun

You are the opposite of a nun

But not the opposite of me

Two things, slightly slanted from each other in time we are

Two things, slightly turned

We are two fists slightly different from one another on one hand

Girl, we are so slightly different

I wonder how we would fare in a room full of nuns

All communing in our feminine vicissitude

Red sky of light coming in and the room expanding

In the grace and holiness that is characteristic of the God

Becoming so great before you, you can't help but give in

Awe? No, that is not at all what I mean

I do not mean to reiterate every small thought I have ever had for all eternity

I mean to suggest that there is one law among many governing all of us

I mean to suggest there is one dakini governing the whole stack of cards

That suggest love

I mean to say there is one female force connecting everything on this earth

So that we cannot see the particularities

But only see the differences

Which are small and wise and interesting to look at

No purpose in it

Oh, quite the contrary, my love

Who fishes on the grand scale in a sea of words

No no there is purpose in it

The purpose though is different than you expected

The purpose is no more simple than to live

I HATE IRONY

I was walking along one day when I realized that I hate irony
I think I was thinking of the movie *The Shining* and how scary it is
When I was 21 I didn't sleep for two nights straight because of that movie
It reminded me a lot of growing up and the things I've seen
Fear is not irony
If you have ever been truly scared there is no irony in your voice when you
    scream
And too
Love is not either
I was in love once and all I could think of was joy
Not drinking, nor sex, or spaghetti
Not witty things to say or martinis
That bubble down the stairs with gracious olives
I didn't think of my large grey turtleneck folding over my abdomen
As I was touched so quietly by the stars
I hate when people think they are being funny by being ironic
Or they want to show you they are clever
So they say something really meaty
With twists and curves
I don't think it is funny to be so elitist
To everyone who hasn't had the chance to be as special as you are
Being cultivated into fine things when you yourself was nothing to begin with
Humor is not irony as I belly laugh all along the bench
Of the waiting room while they announce my father will die
Or when my friend was killed by her husband while he wore all black
To be torched is not ironic, but it hurts
It hurt her flesh. It hurts me to think about it.

And not precious I am to think about it, to give it time
Oh but Dottie, you say, you are so funny
Surely you realize you are always being ironic
But I am not, I will tell you
I am only being real

POETS, YOU ARE EAGER

Young poets, you are so eager
To call the language
That comes after language
That of false children.
Maybe we are not so much false children
As we are conduits of the truth.
The death of the author never meant
The landscaped moon-earth you inhabit
Alongside the strange animals you let in there.
The real life is wild and the animals will bite you.
It is not so much moonless as the moon is seen nowhere
And always felt.
It is no matter, however
As you are just about to eat the fire you speak.
Even now, I can feel the heat upon you
And smell it singe your human flesh

STYLE IS JOY

Dear Lady of the Winter, style is joy

I am sitting here with my stomach full of love

In New York City, I am ready to board the train

In the morning, my pink bags all packed

With crisp white linens, the things I wear

Not like the time in the morning when I visited the shopkeeper in California

Not the time when I was in California, in the morning light

But love, the true kind

All joy has a little style

That is the one thing that you are forgetting

When you write poems so full of blood and guts

They are so real except they aren't

Because they aren't poems really

And every poem full of blood and guts

Must be stylized to be so

Not the time in the morning when I was crying

But the time in the morning when I wasn't

When I wasn't crying

Cause I knew I had found true love

Not the empty truth when I was empty

But the full truth when I wasn't

When I wasn't empty enough to have a stylized shell

Not your empty life you write down with no mediation

But a full life full of love

That I write down with partial mediation

Not the whole truth of bitterness with no bitter shell

But a full life of bitterness with no empty shell

But a joyous and colorful one

But a black one so black
It is hard and fast
Honed by years of thinking
I mean years of thinking
Not anger or sadness
Not bitterness in the morning with some fat slob in California who loves
    his girlfriend
Not the empty sadness of three days fucking some empty slob who loves
    his girlfriend
I am talking about Sunday sadness with ties and ribbons
I am talking about a life of being beaten and then a day spent in costumes
I am talking about children, the children
Who cry out in their stylized laughs
At what a great grand world this is
So pretty in its sunshine that comes on down
On you when you are ready to receive it
The concentrated yellows of bluish sunshine
The sunshine on your face and neck
Your party dress, French vignettes in Egypt
Spent all night wrapped up in tight verse
And underneath
All the crescendos of language
That couldn't show you things more real
Than when they are smart to do so
In rhymes so pretty that they hurt
The sunshine that is so yellow
It comes from a tight yellow sun
That sits, a freakish circle
Packed and wound with painful circuits
Of light, the wires of black and orange

That tight yellow orb we see spilling

It is sitting as simply

As one yellow pebble

On fire so much that it is solid and simple

Just one yellow circle so solid and simple

Cause it is on fire so ferociously that it cannot be bothered

To raise a fuss

I am talking about one yellow circle

On fire so much

In the plastic blue sky

That it is joy

Real joy

Stylized and static joy

The kind that comes only from the moon

The kind of plastic joy that comes only from the moon

Or the greater heavens we can't imagine

They are so vast

They might as well be called joyous.

Even when we try to explain them

The only thing we can say in their vastness

Is something simple

THE POETRY THAT IS GOING TO MATTER AFTER YOU ARE DEAD

Sylvia Plath is my favorite poet. She was not only a descendant of Modernism and the Romantics, she was a poet that cared about her own feelings so much that she cared about yours. She had some fucked-up shit happen in her life, but who cares about that? We all suffer and that has everything to do with poetics. Have you ever heard of Modernism? The Nazis called Modernism primitive and the work of the brutes. The only brutes on this earth are the dogs and those are the things that I love. Do you wonder what I am? You are reading the work of a great poet, possibly one of the greatest ones of your time. If I am standing in front of you right now, you are listening to the voice of one of the greatest poets of your time. Do you take time to analyze greatness? I don't think you should bother—you will never get it right. I am both a Modernist and a Romantic. All poetry that is good today is some combination of modernism, romanticism, ethics, and faith. Take note. All poetry that matters today has feelings in it. You can refute or deny this with your lack of them. You can wrestle against feelings and make funny words for it. Take a look in the mirror. You were born a child and you will die one, too. When you are in your grave all that you will be able to say is mommy. You are going to die you know and so am I. That's it. You were born to die. Take the things you say because you can't write poems and figure out how to write some. Go to the grocery store and buy some food. Sit alone by yourself and think of how it is, the way it really is. There are a million cells of fluid rushing in your veins. On earth a thousand rivers rush through. The only thing that keeps you contained is the faith God has in your every breath. When you are mean, you let him down, so don't be. Read Plath. Hell, read Stein. She was a woman and she would have approved of you—you man, you woman, you dog. Bark your last breath while we all swim along a river. There are children playing around you. They know more than you will ever know.

THE BODY

[FOR ISH KLEIN]

Eric says all my dreams are in my body

All my bad dreams

About betrayal

I don't want to be in this body anymore

That holds all the betrayal of the universe

Its tissues bluing all day into a blue-black

Blood balloon

One day all that blood will be dark and grey

I want to be an unearthly body instead of this one

I want to be a body that is free of dreams

The imagination

I never wanted the imagination within my legs and arms anyway

Blacking within it like forgotten light

Umbrella limbs full of potential light

I never wanted to be the person who tells you

That I believe in you

So that you never had to listen to anyone else

I never wanted

You to forget about me

Freeze me into arctic lust

Until I am never the body

That is amber in the sun

The people, I never wanted the people

To touch my body like they owned it

In dreams

On earth

In real life

I wanted people to believe in my body for once
Not my dreams
That you can walk through in wonderment
Because they are so beautiful
The whole world, the people
They never believed in my body
They only ever believed in their own bodies
Walking and talking
Through the world
Mimetic knights
The people
They only ever believed in their own similar bodies
They only ever believed in the things that were similar
They only ever believed in the cold

CITYSCAPE

I was walking
Through the city
But really I was
Talking to him
But the talking was
In my mind
The metal sky
Was everywhere
I saw the clothing
Store where I had
Lost my head
Everyone said
That she seemed
Annoying
But I knew
She must be sweet
On some level
He only likes
Sweet things
And when I walk through
The sad city
I get chocolates
For him even though
He doesn't love me
Anymore
Still, he never did
Nor does he love
The moon

In the city lights
The moon is gone
But do I care
The moon never
Gave me much
Anyway I remember
Kisses in front
Of the moon
That were
Beleaguered
Am I supposed to only
Love when it is
Time to? Am I supposed
To be there for people
Only when it is time to? My mom calls
Then she forgets I am her daughter. I never
Forget who I love, the place
I am walking in. I never
Forget my head is beating blood
Everywhere. I never forget
How sweet the smile of
The thing you love
And how horrible
The face of the predator.
I wake and walk but
I am always alone and
I can't seem to see
Why this is so bad
But still I want a true
Love. Still I want the

Things that the lovers
Face by the stream
When the moon
Is out. No metal sky
Anywhere. No city
But it is not the city
That is the problem

I DON'T REMEMBER THE TALK OF MEN

I don't remember the words of men that talk
I don't remember the words of men who have led me
From beach to bed
I don't remember
The talk of men, their bitter talk
I don't remember the bitter lemons that have left
The talk of men
I don't remember the bitter lemons
I don't remember
The yellow rinds that have left my mouth
And gone to yours
I don't remember the bitter lemons
I don't remember the talk, the talk of men
Talk is wet
After all
Talk is wet and washes away thusforth
Talk is wet and it washes away
From my mouth into yours
And talk is wet and we are wet too
Talk is wet
I don't remember the bitter lemons

THE LIVING ROOM

The living room did not exist
I wanted to go and lie on the carpet
In the middle of the afternoon
I knew the carpet was dark grey
And in the afternoon sun, I would take a nap
But the room did not exist
It was gone like everything else
In its place was a black bird
That flew and flew
Through the sunlit heavens
With bitter songs in its head
That sounded like two tin cups
Ringing round the world
Intergalactically the world does not seem so large
When things leave as they do
It is not so
What it was before
It is not so large
The black starry dome
Is a room you sit in and smoke hash
What is hash?
I don't even like drugs
What I am trying to say is this:
A great red universe exists and I can't get to it
Somewhere there is a home for me
And I can't ever find it
O Lord, please let me find it
I have been willing to fly anywhere

On a jet plane to get anywhere
On a spaceship I would board with
My suitcase and dog, her head ringing with yellow stars
And rung around a great heart
That keeps popping like a red balloon
Somewhere there is a room
Where I can sleep the whole day
And when I wake everything will be so snug
I am what I awake into
I am what needs to be wrung
From a soaking wet thing
Touch my lips and they are damp
With glistening joy
That was once like stars
But is now something like a forest

I JUST FEEL SO BAD

I just feel so bad
I don't know
How to overcome it
Skinner says that it is my
Way that makes me function
In this world
I like to think
About things that are nice
And pretty
I like to plant purple flowers in my mind
That dazzle the starscape
There is no one for me to talk to
Except you dear reader
When there is no one else
To love, there is only you
To pour my love into
The snow
Echoes out the landscape
I have no home
No bread
I am destitute
But inside me
Is a little voice
That must speak
It gets louder when you listen

NONE OF IT MATTERS

None of it matters, lost one
In the world
None of it matters
I went from water to waterfall
Green world to red world
I went from a world full of deer
To a world full of bears
The tissued world
To a world that was off set
I set the curtains
They said, Set the curtains
So I set the curtains
I spent August in bed
In the same clothes
I kept on the same clothes
For ten weeks
I changed my outfits
Five times a day
And no one listened
I got lost, I got found again
I was always lost
I will always be lost
I will never win at this game
I will never
Be the speaking thing they made me to be
I am not pronouns
Nor am I all of them
I am no I

I wander
And it doesn't matter
I stay the course
I am a star-filled night
Among the unforgivable
I live within a grey world
Within a pretty one
Within one they made for me
I help you find your books
I made the books
I made them, world I held within me
It was no help
I looked at the world with dark eyes
In front of a grey house
I was always lost
In that house
I was always lost, a zero
Am I lost for good?
Shoot I don't know
Mathematical laundress
Of the forgotten egret
I am
Glue me to ten sheets of paper
So that my skin sticks upon them
Write six blue letters upon my skin
I am all object
Throw me around the sky
And I will glisten, a red ball
Floating over buildings and boats
And the sun itself

Hang me on the moon
I am funny-shaped so far away
Stick me where the bunnies go
Let me lie there with them
And those awful ears upon me
Who knows within them
The secrets I will tell

YOU ARE NOT DEAD

I would love you if you were dead
But you are not dead you are alive
You body ringing in me, ringing true
Ringing true, not like a blue nerve net
Encased in glass
Not a red rubber heart encased in glass
Not a burned out body encased in glass
But a real thing, a soft thing
A soft and wild thing
I am so glad I left the world
And found the wildness beyond in you
I am so glad I was brave enough
To leave the place in me that was not wild
To go into the cave of life that is not dead

GRAVE

Dear father, near the grave where you sit
Is not the grave in Harvard Square, very close
To the school that I go to learn to be a teacher.
In that gravesite, there are small stones
That mark the seats of old senators and lonely wives
Grandfathers and their grandchildren, the mothers with powdery voices
The birds that have left us, the bitter bugs
The bugs that went in the river and now go out
The river bugs, O their green wings that glitter
In the moonlight of the half-eaten tree.
I am the squirrel that climbs up the tree in that grave.
In the grave you sit it is the desert and everywhere the wind goes
Passing through the bellies of the dead like air was food
The bugs they are air bugs and there is no one to grab them
I am so glad that no one can grasp an air bug
Which like the mind enters us only when we are willing
To invest our emotions into something called logic.
Whatever soul we have left when the mind is gone is not your soul
What soul logic that empties out the mouth of air bugs
O the air that leaves the mouth of bugs that does transcend
My heart that speaks only of little hearts
Little red hearts that spill out of the blue cloud by your grave
The smooth red velvet hearts that rain down your gravestone
And wet it with red water, wet the air that leaves the grave
And cleans it slowly with red air.

When you go to the otherworld and they ask you your name
Let those little hearts tell you

ACKNOWLEDGMENTS

Thank you to my family and friends for their care and support. Thank you to Joshua Beckman for his invaluable editorial work on this book and to everyone at Wave Books. Thank you to Logan Ryan Smith, who originally published portions of this book in a chapbook entitled, *Tourmaline* (Transmission Press, 2008). Thank you to Katie Geha and Travis Nichols for inspiring the poem "Go on there, boy," which was published in their exhibition catalogue *Poets on Painters* (Ulrich Museum of Art, 2007). Thank you to *All Small Caps Anthology* for publishing the poem, "I am a politician." Thank you to the *So and So Anthology* for publishing the poem, "You are not dead." Thank you to the editors of *The Gurlesque Anthology* (Saturnalia Press, 2010) for publishing "That one was the oddest one." Thank you to the editors of the following journals for publishing some of the poems in this book in their publications: *APlod*, *A Public Space*, *All Small Caps*, *American Poetry Review*, *Coconut*, *Columbia Poetry Review*, *CUE: A Journal of Prose Poetry*, *diode*, *The Fanzine*, *Forklift Ohio*, *Fou*, *Interval(le)s*, *Knock*, *The Laurel Review*, *Loveless*, *MAKE*, *The New Yorker*, *Octopus*, *Parcel*, *The Paris Review*, *past simple*, *Puppy Flowers*, *Satellite Telephone*, *small town*, *Try*, *Typo*, and *Womb Poetry*.